Abra
Lincoln

SADDLEBACK
EDUCATIONAL PUBLISHING

Saddleback's Graphic Biographies

SADDLEBACK
EDUCATIONAL PUBLISHING
Three Watson
Irvine, CA 92618-2767
Website: www.sdlback.com

ISBN-13: 978-1 59905-211-3
ISBN-10: 1-59905-211-3
eBook: 978-1-60291-574-9

Printed in China

President Abraham Lincoln held the United States together through the crisis of the Civil War. When he signed an order freeing the southern slaves, he changed the war from a fight for survival to a crusade for a rebirth of freedom and equality.

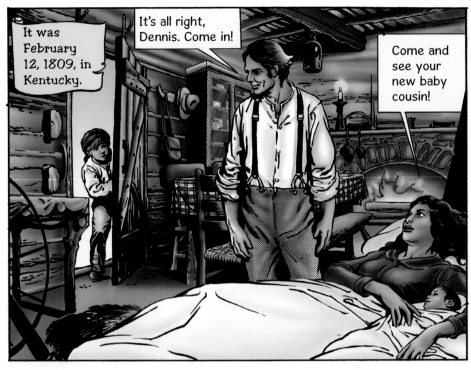

It was February 12, 1809, in Kentucky.

It's all right, Dennis. Come in!

Come and see your new baby cousin!

What are you going to name him, Cousin Nancy?

Abraham, after his grandpa. Abraham Lincoln.

Gosh! He's so little!

Don't worry, Dennis, someday he'll be a big man.

Abe did grow. In a few years he was planting corn ...

... and guiding a plow horse ...

... and gathering wood.

Sometimes he and his sister went to school.

We're lucky there's a school. Lots of people never learn readin' and writin'.

You're smart! You're learning it quick!

The only book the Lincoln's owned was the Bible. He read every word.

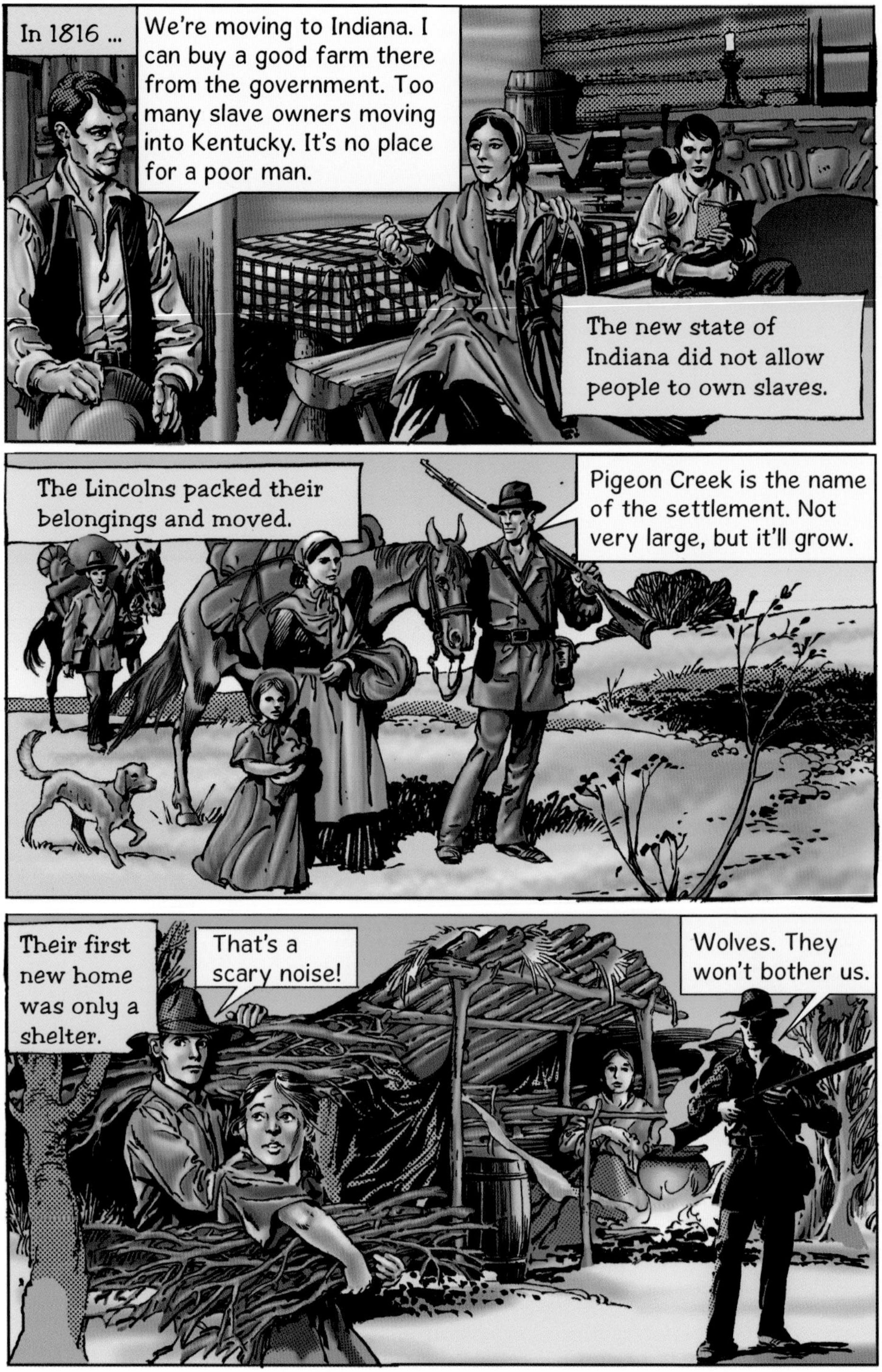
In 1816 ...
We're moving to Indiana. I can buy a good farm there from the government. Too many slave owners moving into Kentucky. It's no place for a poor man.
The new state of Indiana did not allow people to own slaves.
The Lincolns packed their belongings and moved.
Pigeon Creek is the name of the settlement. Not very large, but it'll grow.
Their first new home was only a shelter.
That's a scary noise!
Wolves. They won't bother us.

In the next few years Abe worked harder than ever, helping to clear land for crops and to build a cabin.

With our crops in and a cabin built, things will soon be a bit easier.

But the next year a bad sickness came.

They call it the milk sickness. Some of our neighbors have died of it.

Abe's mother caught it.

I declare, I feel so weak and hot. I don't know what the matter is!

They did all they could, but Nancy Lincoln died.

Sally tried to take her mother's place.

We're out of candles, and I don't know how to make them. We're out of soap, and I don't know how to make soap, so everything's dirty ...

Oh, Abe!

You're doing your best ... you're only a little girl! The worst thing is just missing our mother!

One day Tom Lincoln rode away.

Did Pa say where he was going?

Not a word.

Pa's been gone for days! Do you think anything bad has happened?

I don't know. There are lots of dangers for a lone rider in the forest.

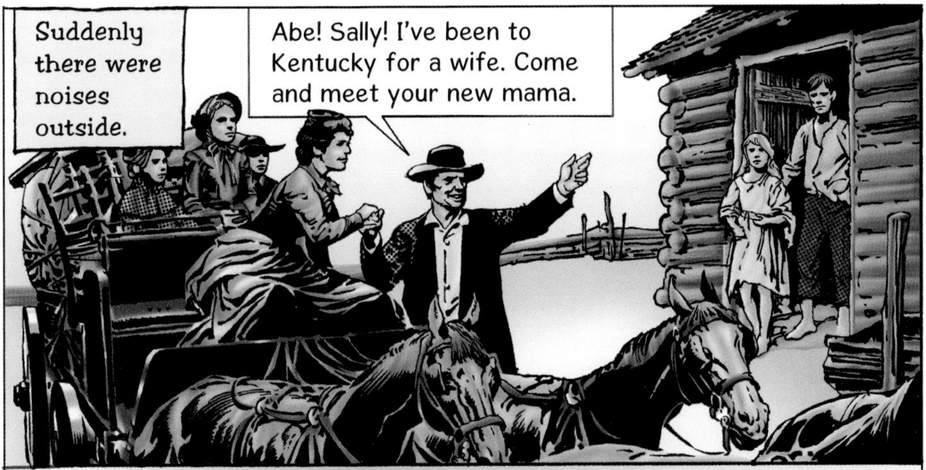
Suddenly there were noises outside.
Abe! Sally! I've been to Kentucky for a wife. Come and meet your new mama.

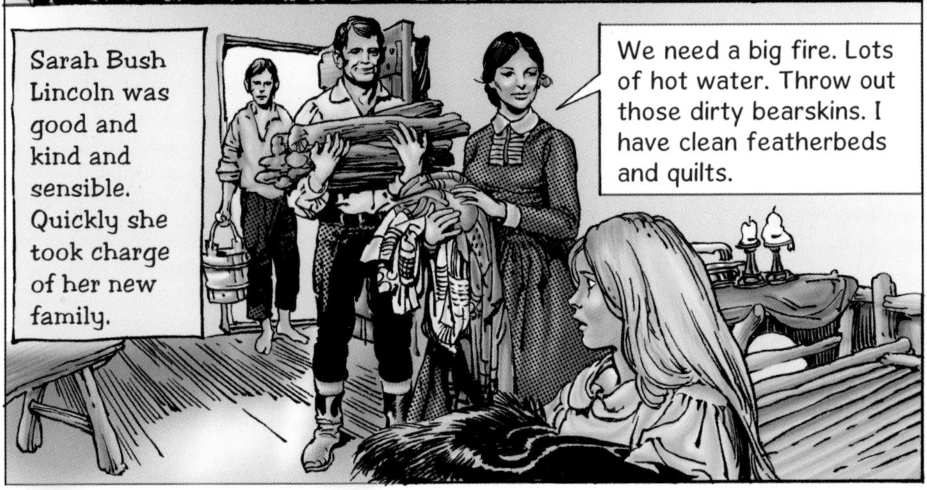
Sarah Bush Lincoln was good and kind and sensible. Quickly she took charge of her new family.
We need a big fire. Lots of hot water. Throw out those dirty bearskins. I have clean featherbeds and quilts.

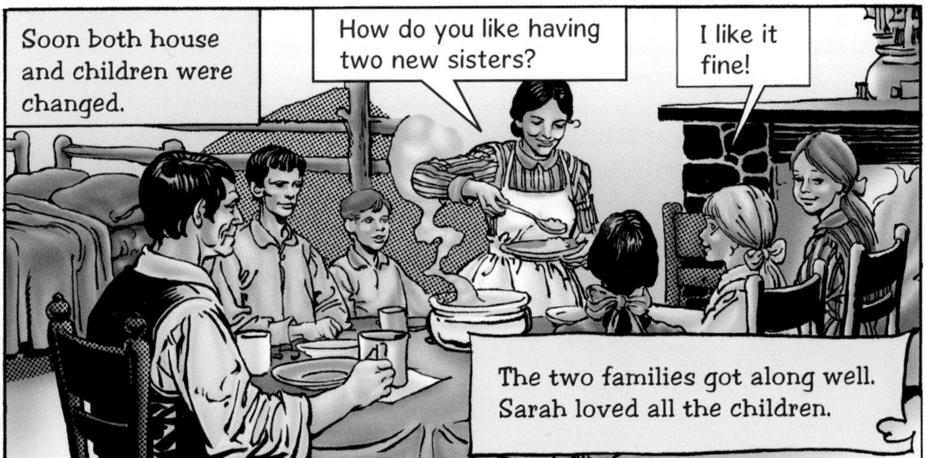
Soon both house and children were changed.
How do you like having two new sisters?
I like it fine!
The two families got along well. Sarah loved all the children.

But Abe was her special favorite.

I'm glad you like to read, son. I wish I knew how.

Oh, yes! I want to know so much, and everything I want to know is in books!

But there were not many books around.

My best friend's a man who can give me a book I ain't read.

He would walk miles to borrow one ...

Thank you, Mr. Pitcher! I'll take the best care of it.

Glad to help anybody who'll walk thirty miles to read a book!

JOHN PITCHER LAWYER

... and get up early or stay up late to have time to read it.

I'll cuff you good if you don't get up and go to work! A boy your age wasting time on such foolishness!

And then ...

That new neighbor's opening a school next winter. I want the children to go.

The younger ones maybe but not Abe! I can hire him out to split fence rails.

Until a boy was 21 years old his wages belonged to his father.

But he's the one who wants it most. And he'll make the most of it!

He can already read and write and figure! Anything more is foolishness! And we need the money!

All in all, Abe never went to school more than a year altogether.

But he would walk 15 miles to the county courthouse.

What are you doing here, Abe?

I learn a lot listenin' to the lawyers argue their cases.

And most nights he went to the crossroads store.

The Louisville paper came today, Abe. The fellows are waitin' to hear you read out the news.

Nothing I'd like better.

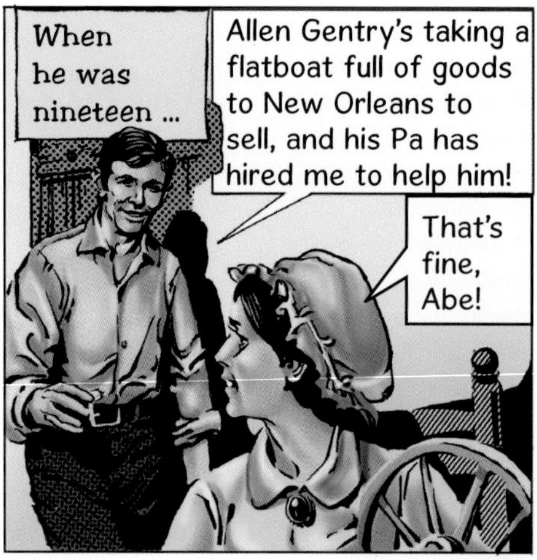
When he was nineteen ...
Allen Gentry's taking a flatboat full of goods to New Orleans to sell, and his Pa has hired me to help him!
That's fine, Abe!

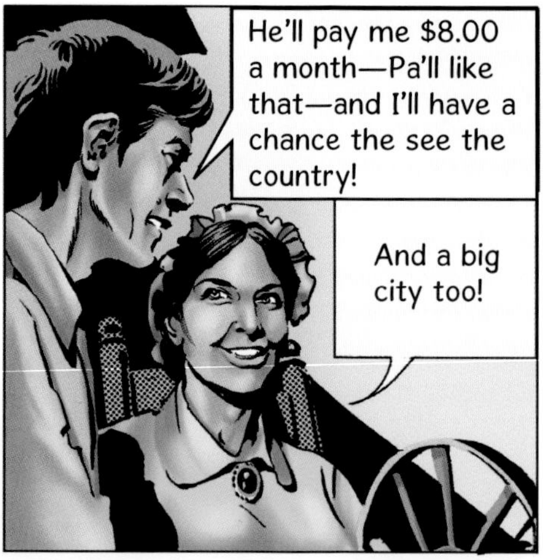
He'll pay me $8.00 a month—Pa'll like that—and I'll have a chance the see the country!
And a big city too!

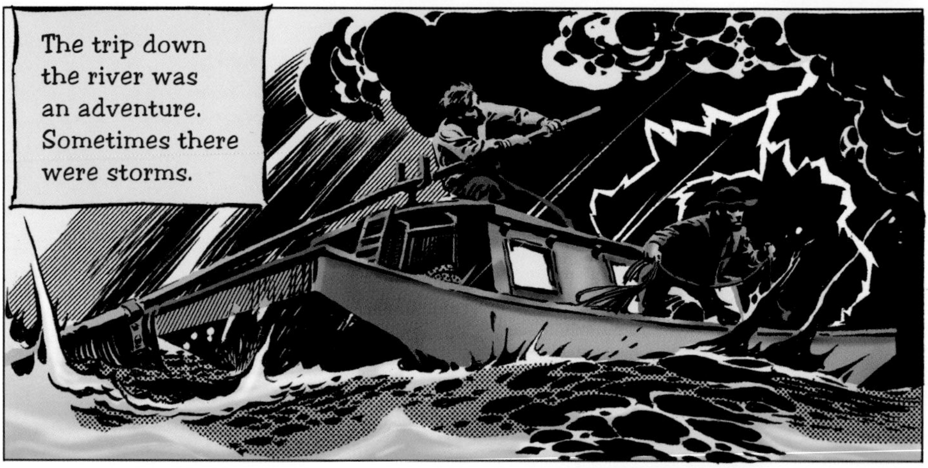
The trip down the river was an adventure. Sometimes there were storms.

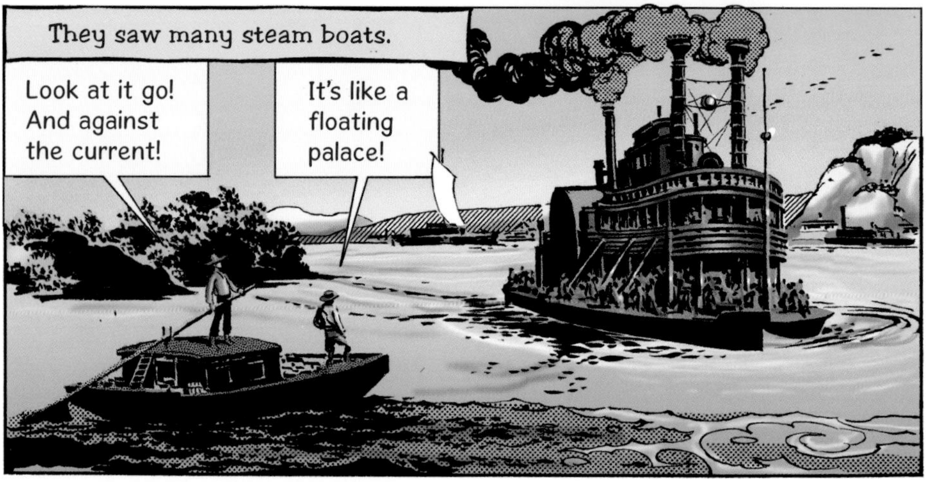
They saw many steam boats.
Look at it go! And against the current!
It's like a floating palace!

The New Orleans waterfront was like a foreign country.

They saw great churches ...

So different from the log meeting house at home!

... beautiful homes ...

How's that for a nice little cabin?

... and a slave auction.

What am I bid? Do I hear five hundred dollars?

Let's go! I can't stand this!

People oughtn't to be sold like animals!

It's not against the law here. They're property.

I'm thankful it's against the law in Indiana. It's not right for one man to own another!

The trip down river had taken a month. After the goods were sold, they returned home in a week by steamboat.

There's Rockport, Abe! We're almost home!

It was good of your Pa to let me make this trip. I'll never forget it!

Abe worked for his father for two more years. Then ...

We're moving, son ... to Illinois. Do you want to come along? You can do what you like, now that you're twenty-one.

I'll come too, long enough to help you get settled.

They traveled by ox-cart. Abe helped to build a new cabin and fence on ten acres of land.

Then ...

Ma, I've got a job in New Salem keeping store for $15 a month. I'm leaving.

I'll miss you, Abe. But it's right for you to go.

In his new job and his new town, Abe soon made friends.

He walked six miles to return six cents he'd overcharged me! I call him "Honest Abe."

When I've no menfolk around, Abe Lincoln carries water from the river for me.

Abe Lincoln's not only the smartest man in the country—he can outrun and out jump and out wrestle all the rest!

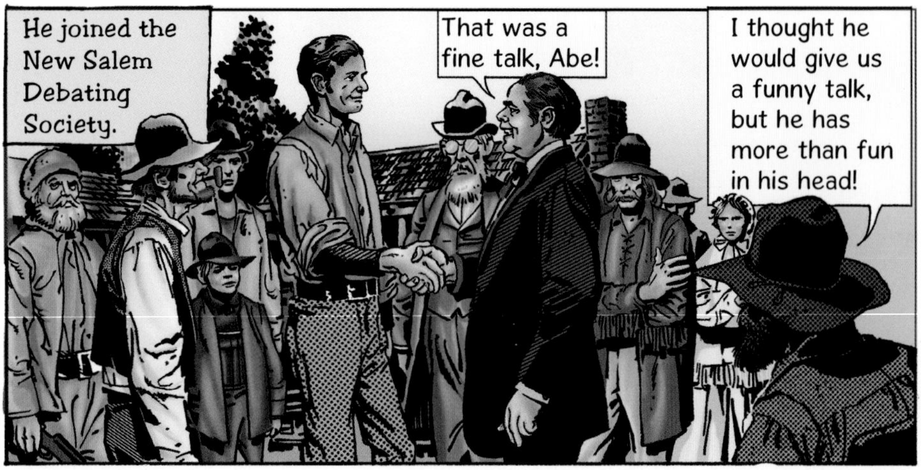
He joined the New Salem Debating Society.
That was a fine talk, Abe!
I thought he would give us a funny talk, but he has more than fun in his head!

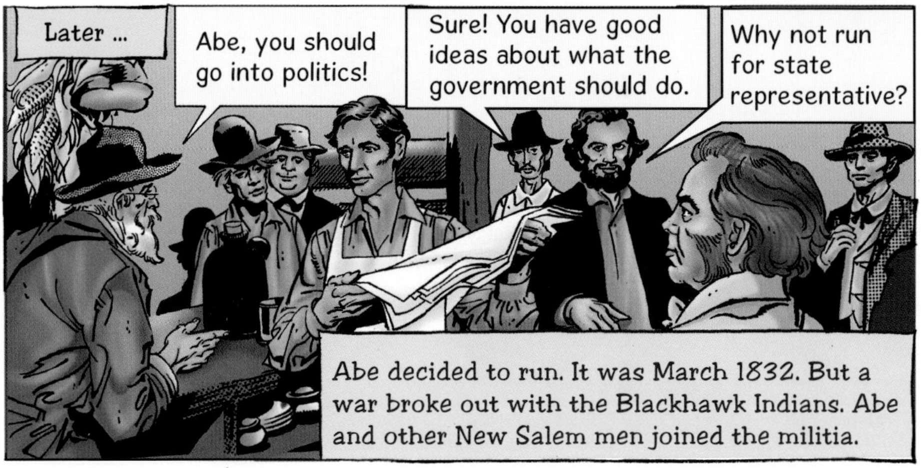
Later ...
Abe, you should go into politics!
Sure! You have good ideas about what the government should do.
Why not run for state representative?
Abe decided to run. It was March 1832. But a war broke out with the Blackhawk Indians. Abe and other New Salem men joined the militia.

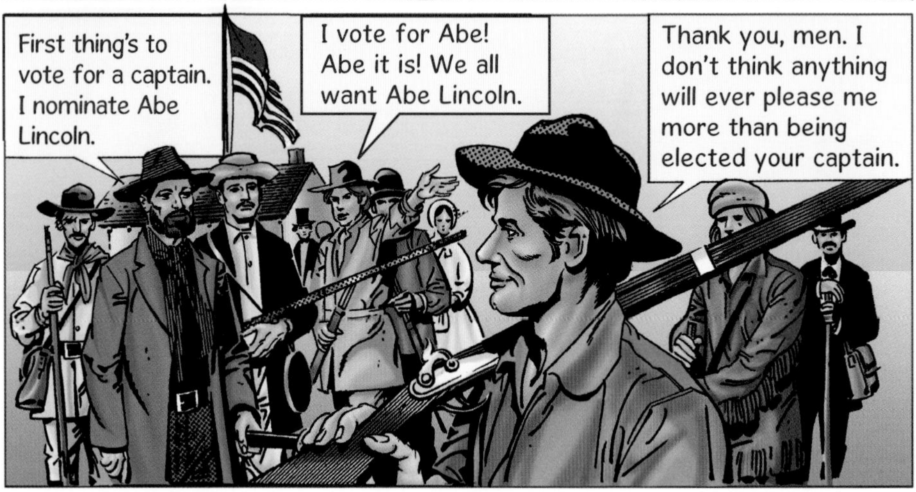
First thing's to vote for a captain. I nominate Abe Lincoln.
I vote for Abe! Abe it is! We all want Abe Lincoln.
Thank you, men. I don't think anything will ever please me more than being elected your captain.

When the war was over, it was only two weeks before the election. Abe lost.

You got a lot of votes, Abe.

Everybody who knew you voted for you. There just wasn't time for you to talk to enough people.

He also studied law.

In 1837 when he was 28-years-old, he got a lawyer's license.

Before the next election in 1834, Abe had time to talk to people and make speeches.

We need better roads and public schools. Every child should have a chance to go to school!

That year he won the election.

He left New Salem for Springfield, the state capital, to enter a law office.

Welcome, Abe! We'll change that to Stuart and Lincoln!

Soon he had many new friends. One night he went to a dance.

Mr. Lincoln, I want you to meet my sister, Mary Todd, from Kentucky.

Miss Todd, I want to dance with you in the worst way!

Abe was not a very good dancer.

Ouch! Ooof!

Excuse me! I'm sorry!

The dance ended.

Mr. Lincoln, you got your wish. You danced with me in the worst way!

But Mary Todd did not really care how Abe danced. She was pretty and popular, but it was Abe she fell in love with. She believed in him.

She wrote to a friend ...

I said once I would marry a man who would be president of the United States. Now I have met the man. He is Abe Lincoln.

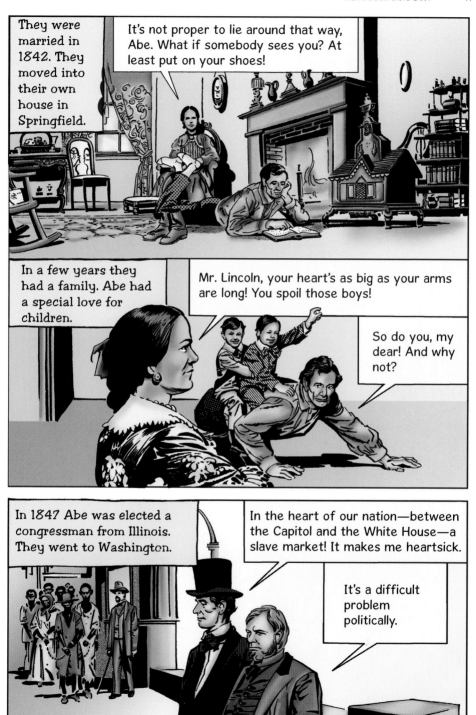

They were married in 1842. They moved into their own house in Springfield.

It's not proper to lie around that way, Abe. What if somebody sees you? At least put on your shoes!

In a few years they had a family. Abe had a special love for children.

Mr. Lincoln, your heart's as big as your arms are long! You spoil those boys!

So do you, my dear! And why not?

In 1847 Abe was elected a congressman from Illinois. They went to Washington.

In the heart of our nation—between the Capitol and the White House—a slave market! It makes me heartsick.

It's a difficult problem politically.

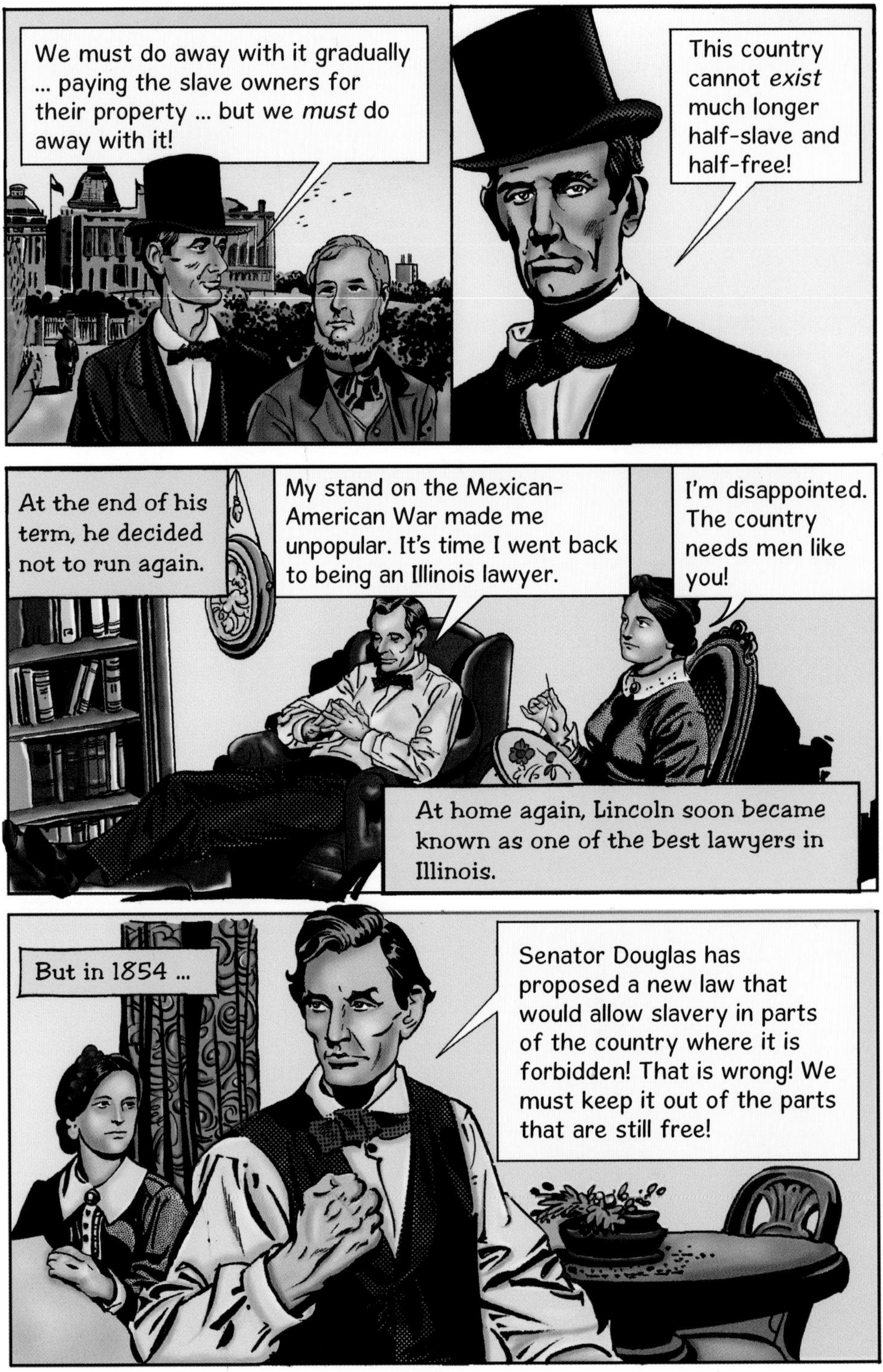
We must do away with it gradually ... paying the slave owners for their property ... but we *must* do away with it!
This country cannot *exist* much longer half-slave and half-free!
At the end of his term, he decided not to run again.
My stand on the Mexican-American War made me unpopular. It's time I went back to being an Illinois lawyer.
I'm disappointed. The country needs men like you!
At home again, Lincoln soon became known as one of the best lawyers in Illinois.
But in 1854 ...
Senator Douglas has proposed a new law that would allow slavery in parts of the country where it is forbidden! That is wrong! We must keep it out of the parts that are still free!

Lincoln began making speeches against slavery.

If the Negro is a man, then my faith teaches me that all men are created equal!

He was asked to run for the Senate against Douglas.

Very well, I'll run. And I'll dare Douglas to debate me in public on the issues!

Douglas agreed. The debates were held in several different towns in Illinois. They were big events.

The long and the short of it!

The Little Giant and Abe, the Giant Killer!

Douglas won the election for Senator. But the debates made Lincoln known all over the United States.

In 1860 he was nominated for president by a new political party, the Republicans.

Douglas will be running against me as a Democrat.

This time you'll win! You will be president!

He had letters from old and new friends.

A little girl from New York State wrote me that I would look better, and win the women's support, if I grew a beard!

Maybe she's right.

And soon Abe started growing a beard.

He traveled around the country campaigning, but on election night, November 6, he was in Springfield.

You're elected! Congratulations, Mr. President!

My wife is at home and will want to hear the news.

The town exploded with happiness.

But when the southern states heard of Lincoln's election ...

We declare that the bond between South Carolina and other states under the name of "The United States of America" is now ended.

By February, seven states had withdrawn from the United States to form a separate government.

On March 4, 1861, Lincoln was sworn in as president and made a speech. He spoke again and again to the people.

I have no purpose, directly or indirectly, to interfere with slavery in the states where it exists. I have no lawful right to do so.

In your hands, my dissatisfied fellow countrymen, and not in mine, is the momentous issue of civil war!

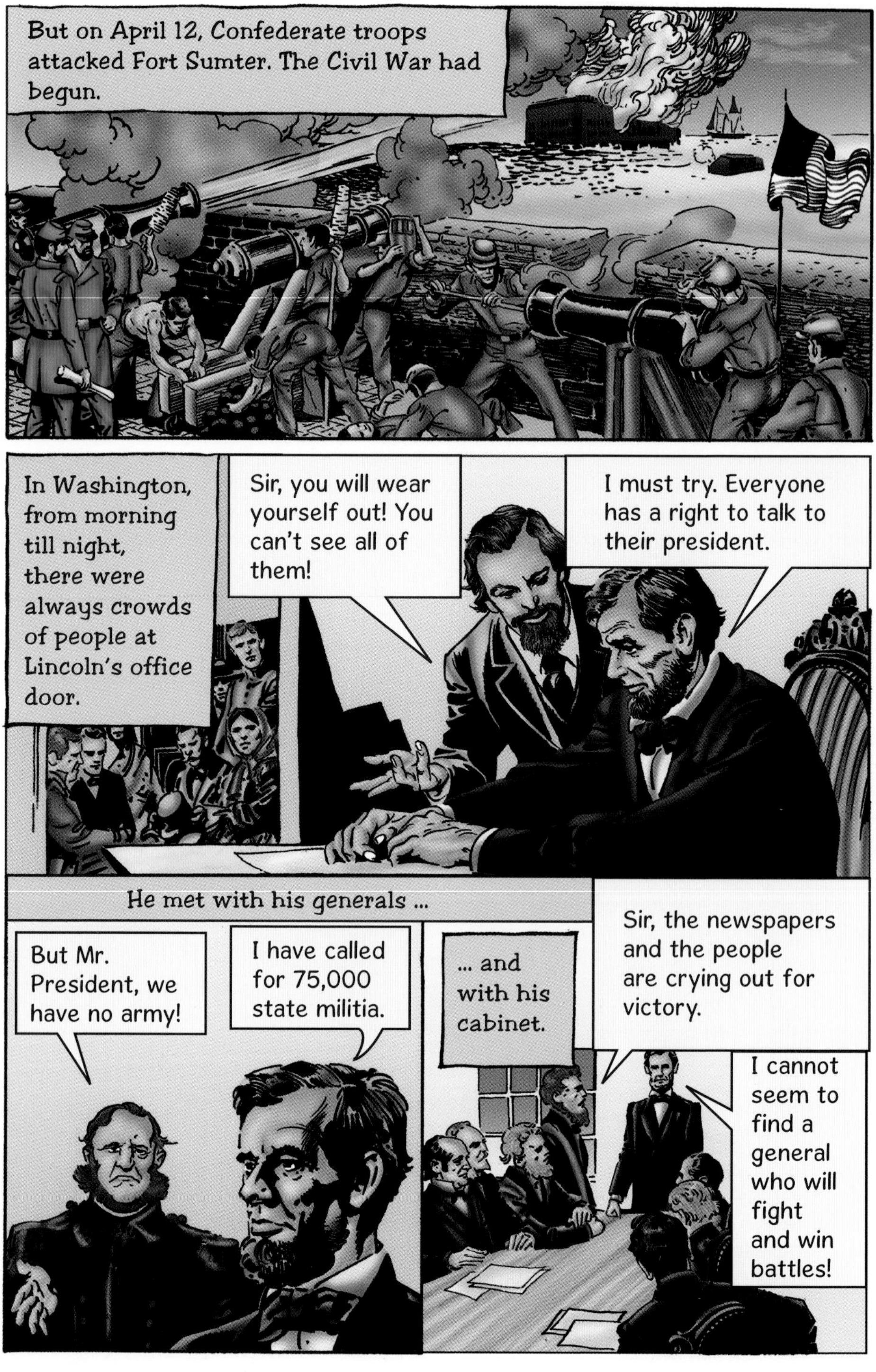
But on April 12, Confederate troops attacked Fort Sumter. The Civil War had begun.
In Washington, from morning till night, there were always crowds of people at Lincoln's office door.
Sir, you will wear yourself out! You can't see all of them!
I must try. Everyone has a right to talk to their president.
He met with his generals ...
But Mr. President, we have no army!
I have called for 75,000 state militia.
... and with his cabinet.
Sir, the newspapers and the people are crying out for victory.
I cannot seem to find a general who will fight and win battles!

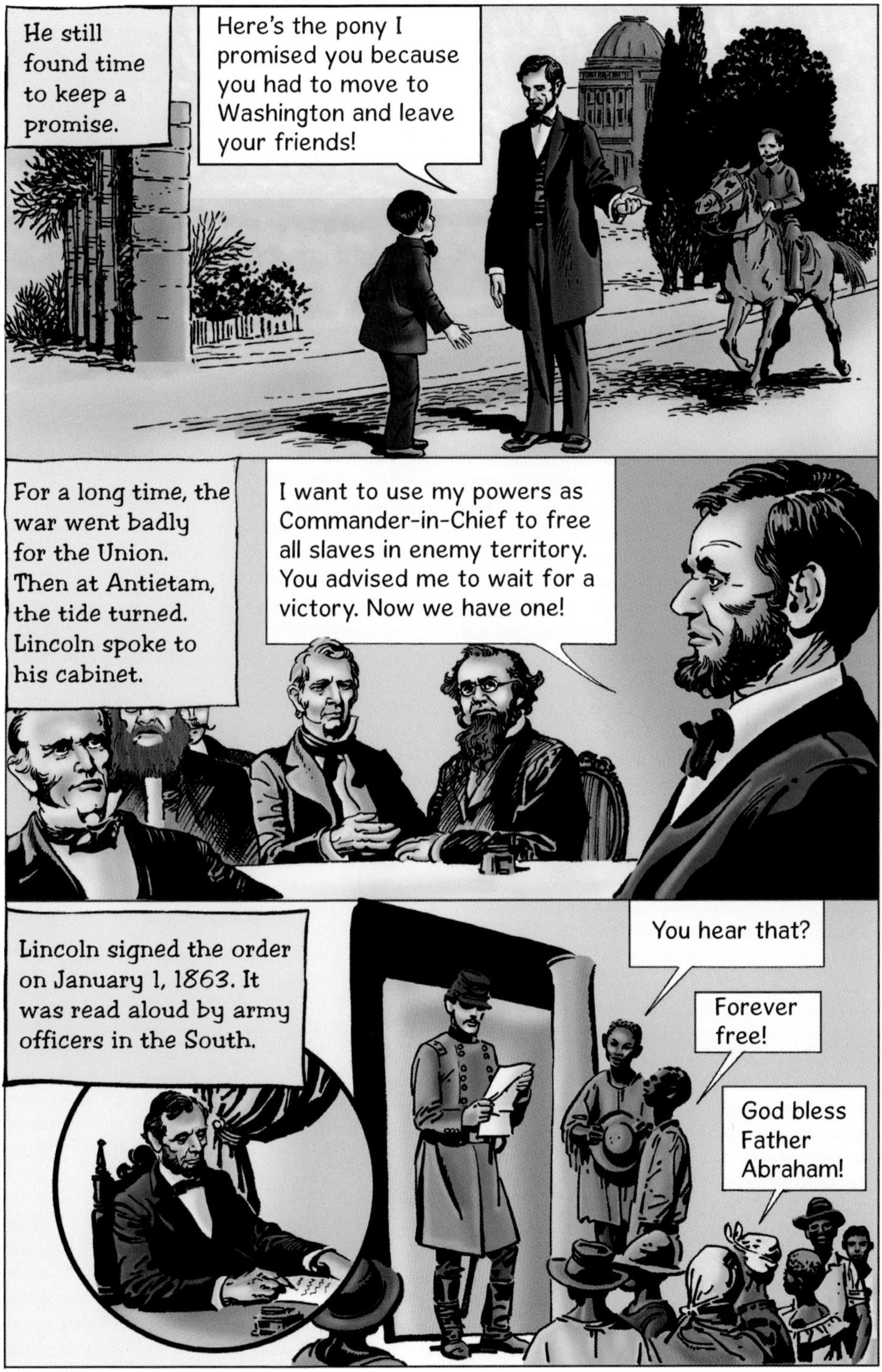
He still found time to keep a promise.
Here's the pony I promised you because you had to move to Washington and leave your friends!
For a long time, the war went badly for the Union. Then at Antietam, the tide turned. Lincoln spoke to his cabinet.
I want to use my powers as Commander-in-Chief to free all slaves in enemy territory. You advised me to wait for a victory. Now we have one!
Lincoln signed the order on January 1, 1863. It was read aloud by army officers in the South.
You hear that?
Forever free!
God bless Father Abraham!

Lincoln was re-elected and at his inauguration on March 7, 1865, he made another speech.

With malice toward none, with charity for all ... let us strive on to finish the work we are in, to bind up the nation's wounds.

On April 9, the Confederate army surrendered.

The fighting is over. The killing is ended! Thank God I lived to see it.

A few nights later, they went to the theater.

A crazed southern actor crept to the door of the president's box.

The man, John Wilkes Booth, fired— then jumped to the stage.

Stop him! He shot the president!

The president's wound was fatal. He died without becoming conscious again.

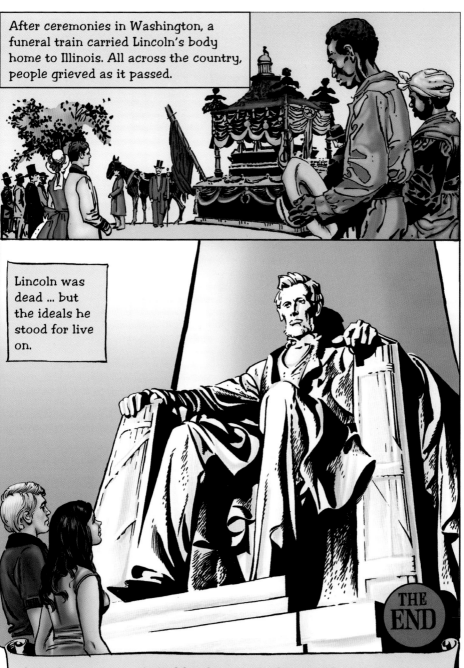

After ceremonies in Washington, a funeral train carried Lincoln's body home to Illinois. All across the country, people grieved as it passed.

Lincoln was dead ... but the ideals he stood for live on.

THE END

As he became a symbol of freedom, so the Lincoln Memorial in Washington has become a gathering place for those who work to prove that "all men are created equal."

Saddleback's Graphic Fiction & Nonfiction

If you enjoyed this Graphic Biography ... you will also enjoy our other graphic titles including:

Graphic Classics

- Around the World in Eighty Days
- The Best of Poe
- Black Beauty
- The Call of the Wild
- A Christmas Carol
- A Connecticut Yankee in King Arthur's Court
- Dr. Jekyll and Mr. Hyde
- Dracula
- Frankenstein
- The Great Adventures of Sherlock Holmes
- Gulliver's Travels
- Huckleberry Finn
- The Hunchback of Notre Dame
- The Invisible Man
- Jane Eyre
- Journey to the Center of the Earth
- Kidnapped
- The Last of the Mohicans
- The Man in the Iron Mask
- Moby Dick
- The Mutiny On Board H.M.S. Bounty
- The Mysterious Island
- The Prince and the Pauper
- The Red Badge of Courage
- The Scarlet Letter
- The Swiss Family Robinson
- A Tale of Two Cities
- The Three Musketeers
- The Time Machine
- Tom Sawyer
- Treasure Island
- 20,000 Leagues Under the Sea
- The War of the Worlds

Graphic Shakespeare

- As You Like It
- Hamlet
- Julius Caesar
- King Lear
- Macbeth
- The Merchant of Venice
- A Midsummer Night's Dream
- Othello
- Romeo and Juliet
- The Taming of the Shrew
- The Tempest
- Twelfth Night

SADDLEBACK
EDUCATIONAL PUBLISHING